Rocks Not Happy
In Sacks

by Gilbert Walking Bull
and Sally Moore

illustrations
by tom novak

Library of Congress Control Number: 2008926032

Text pre-published in "OH-KU-KA-KAN" (1975, 2006).
Used here by permission of Gilbert Walking Bull.
www.tatankamani.org

ISBN: 978-1-57579-357-7
Distributed by RedGravel Ink

Printed in the United States of America, April 2008.

First Edition

Pine Hill Press
4000 West 57th Street
Sioux Falls, SD 57106

Celebrating

Gilbert Walking Bull

June 16, 1930 - April 7, 2007

... my teacher, my friend.

My dog Gimo

knows rocks

not happy in sacks.

I met my friend, the rock man, in Redmond.

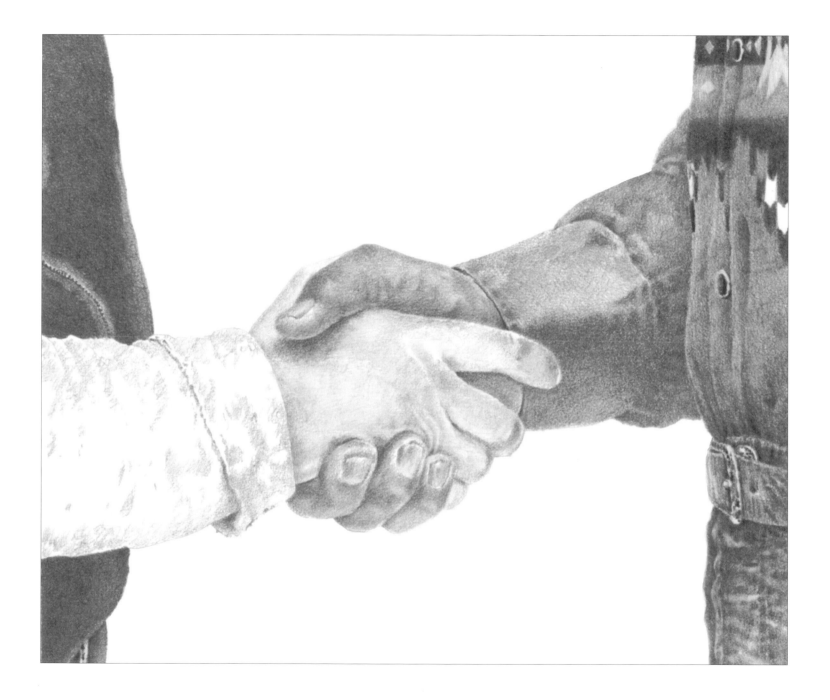

He was from Indiana,
and we talked about
thunder eggs.

Next thing I know
when I get home,
he sends me a
sack of rocks.

These rocks stay
in sack long time,

and I forget I

have them

until Gimo tears

at the sack.

He knows rocks not happy there.

He growls and pulls at the sack,

and it comes to my
mind that rocks
are sacred to my
people,

that rocks **are** people

and belong to the earth.

So I pick up the sack and
look around for a place
for them to rest where
they can be seen.

Now rocks are settled
and happy on the earth,
not closed up in dark
sack anymore.

I put them in the
flower bed near the
window where I can
look out to see them,

and anyone else can see them

getting the sun,

the wind, and the rain.

Each day they look happier.

The poem *Rocks Not Happy In Sacks* first appeared in print in an anthology, <u>O-HU-KAH-KAN</u>. It was written by Gilbert Walking Bull and tells the story of actual events that occurred in his life. The poem demonstrates Gilbert's belief that all of life is sacred, and all of creation is life; *Mitakuye Oyasin*, All my relations.

Gilbert Walking Bull was the lineal descendent of James Moves Camp, a Lakota sacred man. He was also a descendent of Sitting Bull. On his mother's side he was from the band of Crazy Horse and Black Elk. As a child he was kept out of government schools and had very little exposure to American society or the English language until he was 16 years old. He was raised in the traditional way of the Lakota culture, through the language, ceremonies, stories and songs of the people. Gilbert's gentle manner and deep understanding of the indigenous earth-centered philosophy earned him international recognition as a teacher and spiritual leader.

Sally Moore lives in a little house built into the side of a hill in South Dakota. She worked closely with Gilbert at Tatanka Mani Camp, a community dedicated to preserving the culture of the Lakota people through Gilbert and his teachings. This book is one of the projects they worked on together.

tom novak was born and raised in Chicago where he graduated from the School of the Art Institute of Chicago in 1973 and almost immediately moved out west to Oregon to try his hand at being a cowboy. The cowboying didn't work out but he did stay in Oregon. In 1980 he opened "novak's studio" and has been creating art full time ever since. He has two wonderful sons, Kip and Bram. To see more of tom's work please visit his website: www.novakstudio.com.